W9-BMJ-516

It's New Year's Day!

by Richard Sebra

BUMBA BOOKS™

LERNER PUBLICATIONS ◆ MINNEAPOLIS

Note to Educators:

Throughout this book, you'll find critical thinking questions. These can be used to engage young readers in thinking critically about the topic and in using the text and photos to do so.

Lerner Publications Company
A division of Lerner Publishing Group, Inc.
241 First Avenue North
Minneapolis, MN 55401 USA

For reading levels and more information, look up this title at www.lernerbooks.com.

Library of Congress Cataloging-in-Publication Data

The Cataloging-in-Publication Data for *It's New Year's Day!* is on file at the Library of Congress.
ISBN 978-1-5124-2565-9 (lib. bdg.)
ISBN 978-1-5124-2923-7 (pbk.)
ISBN 978-1-5124-2744-8 (EB pdf)

Manufactured in the United States of America
1 – VP – 12/31/16

LERNER
e
SOURCE

Expand learning beyond the printed book. Download free, complementary educational resources for this book from our website, www.lernerresource.com.

Table of Contents

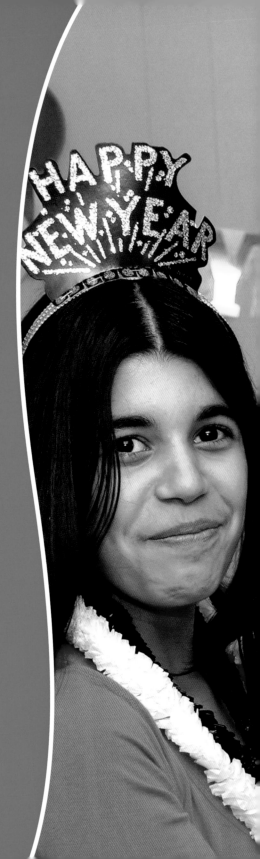

New Year's Day

New Year's Day is

a holiday.

It is January 1.

New Year's Day marks

the beginning of a new

calendar year.

New Year's Day is celebrated around the world. Some people celebrate with fireworks.

The night before New Year's Day

is New Year's Eve.

The new year begins at midnight

on New Year's Eve.

Why does the new year begin at midnight?

A big ball drops

in New York City.

People gather to see it.

They count down the

seconds to midnight.

People celebrate at midnight.

They blow horns.

They throw confetti.

13

On New Year's Day, some families

eat black-eyed peas.

People think that this food brings

good luck.

What do you think are lucky foods?

HAPPY
NEW YEAR

Odd Fellows & Rebekahs

Shining
Still

People meet.

Some people go

to parades.

People share hopes for the new year.

They make New Year's resolutions.

Why do you think people make resolutions?

New Year's Day is a time

to celebrate the past year.

It is also a time to look forward

to the next year.

New Year's Day Calendar

JANUARY

SUNDAY	MONDAY	TUESDAY	WEDNESDAY	THURSDAY	FRIDAY	SATURDAY
					1	2
3	4	5	6	7	8	9
10	11	12	13	14	15	16
17	18	19	20	21	22	23
24	25	26	27	28	29	30
31						

Picture Glossary

confetti

small pieces of colored paper that are thrown at parades and celebrations

eve

the evening or day before an important day

midnight

twelve o'clock at night

resolutions

promises people make to themselves

23

Index

black-eyed peas, 15

calendar year, 4

confetti, 12

horns, 12

midnight, 8, 11, 12

New Year's Eve, 8

New York City, 11

parades, 17

resolutions, 18

Read More

Appleby, Alex. *Happy New Year!* New York: Gareth Stevens Publishing, 2014.

Jules, Jacqueline. *What a Way to Start a New Year!* Minneapolis: Kar-Ben, 2013.

Peppas, Lynn. *New Year's Day.* New York: Crabtree Publishing, 2010.

Photo Credits

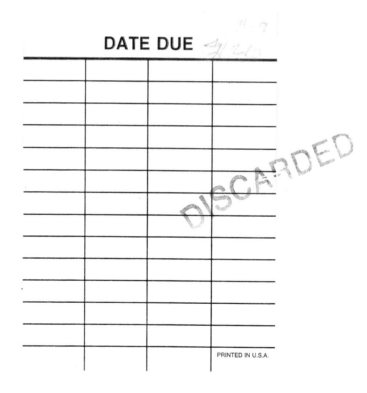

DATE DUE

PRINTED IN U.S.A.